PRAISE FOR
THE BITE-SIZED ENTREPRENEUR

"You can create the life you imagined and still be an entrepreneur. Damon's new book will give you the easy way to implement strategies and do just that. Entrepreneurship is the best gig ever only if you do it the way Damon lays out. Otherwise, you'll be working for the worst boss you ever had."

--Cameron Herold, author of Double Double *and* Meetings Suck

"For every would-be entrepreneur who's wondered if it's possible to "crush it" without crushing yourself, this book is for you! In this concise read, Inc. columnist Damon Brown lays out a road map for launching a satisfying and successful business without overturning the life you currently have."

–Meagan Francis, co-host, the LifeWork Podcast

"Sure, it starts with passion, but what do you know about living the life of an entrepreneur? The Bite-Sized Entrepreneur *gives smart, succinct advice about how to follow your business dreams, including why to treat Tuesday like Monday; the difference between busyness and productivity; and three effective ways of saying 'no.' Highly recommended for would-be entrepreneurs and freelancers."*

--Kelly James-Enger, author of Six-Figure Freelancing, Second Edition: The Writer's Guide to Make More Money

"A practical and actionable guide to accomplishing your goals that can help anyone master the mindset needed to become a self-made success."

–Scott Steinberg, bestselling author of Make Change Work for You

"*In* The Bite-Sized Entrepreneur, *Damon Brown lays waste to both the misconceptions and pesky little lies we tell ourselves about why we can't make our side hustles a reality. A thoughtful, provocative read, Brown will help you understand why you have more time than you think to follow your passions—and offers smart, actionable advice to help you implement the right strategies so you can make your side hustle successful within the boundaries of the life you live today.*"

—Kayt Sukel, *author of* The Art of Risk *and* This Is Your Brain On Sex

Jennifer,

Productivity > Business
Every Time!

All the Best,

[signature]

11/17

THE PRODUCTIVE BITE-SIZED ENTREPRENEUR

BITE-SIZED ENTREPRENEUR BOOK #2
24 SMART SECRETS TO
DOING MORE IN LESS TIME

Damon Brown
Inc.com columnist &
Co-Founder of Cuddlr
www.bitesized.biz

TWITTER/INSTAGRAM: *@BROWNDAMON*
CONSULTING & SPEAKING REQUESTS:
DAMON@DAMONBROWN.NET

PUBLISHED BY:
Damon Brown

The Productive Bite-Sized Entrepreneur,
1st Edition
Copyright 2016 by Damon Brown
Edited by Jeanette Hurt
Cover designed by Bec Loss

*Some material has been graciously reprinted
or inspired by my work on Inc. Magazine
Online, within random tweets, and on
scribbled index cards. Thank you.*

To Abhi,
whose smile reminds me of the beauty of life
itself.
Thank you.

"In fact, there is no inherent problem in our desire to escalate our goals, as long as we enjoy the struggle along the way."

- Mihaly Csikszentmihalyi, Flow

Reading

OTHER BITE-SIZED BOOKS

THE BITE-SIZED ENTREPRENEUR

(KINDLE, AUDIOBOOK ON AUDIBLE & ITUNES)

THE PRODUCTIVE BITE-SIZED ENTREPRENEUR

(PAPERBACK, KINDLE)

Selected Books by the Author

The Bite-Sized Entrepreneur:

21 Ways to Ignite Your Passion &

Pursue Your Side Hustle

Our Virtual Shadow:

Why We Are Obsessed with Documenting Our

Lives Online

Porn & Pong:

How Grand Theft Auto, Tomb Raider

and Other Sexy Games Changed Our Culture

Playboy's Greatest Covers

HOW NOT TO BE PRODUCTIVE

When I wrote the first THE BITE-SIZED ENTREPRENEUR, my intention was to arm you with everything you needed to find and trust your passion, and use that direction to create your ultimate side hustle.

You and other wonderful readers sent me great feedback about your own personal journeys in entrepreneurship, along with your questions. Lots of questions. I quickly realized that you were hungry for more.

I liken it to going to one of those upscale, gourmet Vegas buffets: You can sample just about anything and everything that a restaurant has to offer, but once you've tried it all, you know what food you really love. Once you know what you prefer, your next move should be going straight to a restaurant that specializes in that dish.

THE PRODUCTIVE BITE-SIZED ENTREPRENEUR is specialty served on a platter. If the first book laid the foundation to ignite your passion, this follow-up is here to help you sustain it. After all, once you make room in your life and grow into your successful side hustle, then your main focus has to be on maintaining and strengthening your business. Your business is always a reflection of yourself. This book will make you a more productive version of yourself.

If you are looking for productivity hacks, then this is probably the wrong book for you. It's actually my fault, not just because I wrote this book you have in your hands, but because I have an aversion to the popular word "hack". Part of it is my background, as, in journalism, a hack is someone who is a lazy writer. Part of it is the second life of my career, as a tech entrepreneur, where a hack is a quick, smart shortcut to a problem.

Here's the issue: There is no shortcut to productivity. There is no hack.

In being around extremely productive people and observing my own most productive periods, I've found that strong productivity is less about banal, universal shortcuts and more about preparing your mindset. In culinary culture, preparers do a mis en place, an organization of their tools, raw foods, and other items, just in the right place so that, when order after order comes in at the heat of the night, they don't need to think about what's next. Smart productivity is the same way. It is instinctive from preparation and habit.

I learned this first hand, as my most productive time wasn't 15 years of working 60 hours a week as a freelance journalist and author, but the three years of working 15 hours a week as a journalist, author, entrepreneur, and speaker after my two sons were born. As I said in THE BITE-SIZED

ENTREPRENEUR, "I found myself learning Apple's iPhone programming language with one hand while rocking my newborn in my other, spare arm." The very limitation of time accelerated my productivity, but I also had to be mentally ready to step up my game.

To be the most productive, you have to make room for inspiration, set the plate for action, and give patience for recovery. Keep in mind that inspiration doesn't mean waiting until you feel like doing something, but putting in the proper R & D (research and development) so you are likely to find the creative spark and the strategic genius. Setting the plate is keeping obstacles clear of your momentum. Recovery is respecting your own balance, celebrating your progress, and assessing your next move.

Being productive every single day is a fruitless goal. To maximize productivity, you have to accept that you will not be able to give 100% every single moment of your life. Constantly working means you aren't taking time to integrate lessons learned during action, just as much as staying idle means you aren't testing theories in your head.

Productivity is a cycle, not a sprint.

I call the productivity process "pursuing, doing, and renewing". It is an infinite iterative flow where we research our interests, implement our theories, and assess our growth. It is not unlike Steve Blank's landmark Lean Startup method, in which you ship the "minimal viable product", or MVP, to get feedback from others as much as possible. In the case of productivity, we're getting feedback from ourselves.

THE PRODUCTIVE ENTREPRENEUR is broken down into three sections loosely based on the process: Pursuing, Doing, and Renewing. Like other THE BITE-SIZED ENTREPRENEUR books, you can read the strategies in any order, but your productivity will be much stronger if you go through it from top to bottom. If you are new to entrepreneurial pursuits, it also may be worthwhile reading the original THE BITE-SIZED ENTREPRENEUR to get a solid foundation for the basics.

It would be indulgent to spend more time laying the groundwork for a book on productivity, so let's get started. Enjoy!

-Damon Brown, September 2016

I: PURSUING

"At the beginning of any new idea, the possibilities can seem infinite, and that wide-open landscape of opportunity can become a prison of anxiety and self-doubt."

-Peter Sims, Little Bets

1

CREATE LIMITATIONS

You automatically take as much time as you are given

It began with getting up at 5 a.m. That was the plan. Our baby would wake up at 6, and, since I was the primary caretaker at home, I'd be able to get a sufficient amount of business done before then. I quickly learned that meant I didn't shower unless he took a nap, so I started getting up at 4:30 a.m. Then I realized I couldn't make morning tea or coffee unless I got up at 4:15 a.m., and that I had to refuse my steadily increasing workload unless I woke up at 4:00 a.m.

The scales kept adjusting until I found a new wakeup time: 3:15 a.m. It was an hour after the bar's last call, making it officially morning. Three o' clock still carries the smell and the silence of the night, though, and it gave me the isolation and darkness that fueled my creativity. I traded my extreme late nights of younger years for very productive mornings. I had space.

My son became my end-of-day clock, and when he rang around 6 a.m., I had usually already talked to my New York contacts, written an article, and tackled a new business strategy for my first app, So Quotable. The time shift became invaluable when I launched my app Cuddlr, not only because my main co-founder was in the U.K., but later when I needed significant time to steer its significant userbase and eventual acquisition.

Around the time of my change, I caught a popular article that said we used to sleep in two shifts as recently as a couple centuries ago.

[Virginia Tech History professor Roger Ekirch] found that we didn't always sleep in one eight hour chunk. We used to sleep in two shorter periods, over a longer range of night. This range was about 12 hours

long, and began with a sleep of three to four hours, wakefulness of two to three hours, then sleep again until morning.

That was all I needed to hear. "Maybe this temporary thing will work…forever!" I told myself one morning before sunrise.

After several months, however, I realized that this should not – or rather, could not – be my default. My moods began swinging. My body began to ache.

I told myself to hang in there, that I'd keep at it for a year. As the 12th month arrived on the horizon, I hit the equivalent of a runner's wall, and I limped to the finish line.

Clearly, it was time for a change. I decided to look at my priorities. I started saying no to gigs, accepted that parts of my to-do list wouldn't get done, and gave myself at least one alarm-free morning every week. The aches went away, my mind cleared up, and everything became more focused. The year following this experiment was even more productive, as I zeroed in on only the projects about which I was most passionate – simply because I didn't have the time to do anything else.

My years of working at odd hours and [insert chuckle here] "waiting to be inspired" to create were replaced by a stable, disciplined regiment. In an instant, my 60-hour-work week was sliced down to 15 hours a week. I viewed myself as a marathon runner doing a daily, three-hour leg.

My first year as a parent became one of the most productive years of my life.

Have you ever found yourself more productive when you have less time? It reminds me of an old programming adage: Programmers always manage to get things done with just the amount of computer memory they are given. It's the same reason why we always seem to spend through the money we have, or feel like we complete things just before the deadline is about to strike. We automatically take as much space as we are given.

When we are aware of how much little time we have, though, we begin compressing. As Brain Pickings' Maria Popova shared in a recent article, our relative view of time slows down when we feel threatened. In this case, the threat could be not getting the last sentence down in an idea or not sending out that client email before you run out of time. You realize how many minutes you spend checking social media, fixing a snack, or gazing out of the window. Those moments of disengagement can become the quiet time killers that keep you from being more efficient.

I learned this rather recently. In my compressed work year, I did my first TED talk, gave a keynote speech at

American University, programmed and designed my first app, made TV appearances on Al Jazeera America and other outlets, and joined multiple startup advisory boards – all while being my first son's primary caretaker while still maintaining an active writing career. Not only was I driven by passion for both my family and my work, but also by my acute awareness that time was limited. My proverbial alarm clock was going to wake up around 6 a. m., which, from 3 a. m., gave me about 180 minutes each day to get my passion projects accomplished.

Here are some thoughts on how to maximize your time:

Monotasking

As I discuss in my book *Our Virtual Shadow: Why We Are Obsessed with Documenting Our Lives Online*, scientific studies now prove multitasking doesn't really exist. What we view as multitasking is just picking up one task, dropping it quickly for another task, and then repeating the same process over and over again until they are both done. Instead, concentrate on getting one thing done well. The completion will boost your energy-and focus-for the next item on your list.

Return on investment
Forget the money ROI – what is your time ROI? We lose the most time by wasting it on items that shouldn't be high on our priority list. For all the great opportunities I fulfilled during my compressed year, I said "No" to even more opportunities than I accepted. I still do.

Slice and dice
In her book *Six-Figure Freelancing*, Kelly James Enger talks about breaking the day up into 15-minute segments. This former lawyer gets things done by essentially giving herself a time limit for her work.

Time, not money, is an entrepreneur's most precious resource. A life change taught me this lesson, but you shouldn't wait for that to happen.

2
DEVELOP YOUR CORE
Do many things with one purpose

Have you noticed that the most productive people usually aren't exhausted? I mean, they get tired, but you rarely see them ready to pass out in a random corner or forced to take a mandatory vacation based on doctors' orders. On the other hand, those who seem the most stressed and burnt out seem to get things done within a hair of failure. If the wind blew the wrong way, you'd expect them just to topple over right where they once stood.

You can point to personality, disposition, or stamina, but I believe it comes down to one special difference: Focus. The most productive people are focused, usually on one priority. The least productive people are focused on many things, usually on many priorities, which, of course, means that nothing really is a priority. It is multitasking versus monotasking and diffused energy versus concentrated energy. Have you ever taken a magnifying glass and made a pinpoint with the rays of the sun until smoke started to rise? Productive people bring that level of concentration to their goals.

It gets confusing, though, when the most popular productive people seem to be spread so damn thin. For every creative like Jiro Ono, the singular-focused master chef featured in the film *Jiro Dreams of Sushi*, there are lots more like Richard Branson, the multimedia mogul who has built music, movies, airlines, and even spaceships under his Virgin brand. Oprah Winfrey, Jeff Bezos, and others always seem to have a new venture, yet never seem to be as stretched as much as the average Joe multitasking through his relatively simple life.

The truth is that Jiro and Richard and Oprah and Jeff are the same. Their expressions are obviously different, but they all have one simple, clear intention to their career. That's why it is absolutely crucial that you say "No" as often as possible. Can you imagine how many times Jiro said "No" to expanding beyond his small, exclusive restaurant (watch the movie to get a better idea), or the few number of times Oprah actually says "Yes" to a new project idea?

The beautiful part is that each of these successful individuals instinctually knows what next step for their business should likely be and what would be a misfire – simply because they have taken the time to know themselves and, therefore, found their purpose. Why do you do want to do what you do? If you want to be the most productive, then you have to know your end game.

And, in a Zen-like paradox, the better you know yourself, the less options you have to grow, as everything won't be for you, but the more narrow that focus, the more productive you will be in the areas that you *do* care about.

One of my favorite analogies is from Martha Stewart's *The Martha Rules*. My mentor Andrea King Collier told me about the following excerpt years ago. It ended up changing the course of my career:

We once [listed] all of our media platforms and traced how the little pansy flower had been covered in each one: Our magazine featured cupcakes decorated with sugared pansies; on television, I demonstrated how to apply pressed pansies onto paper, creating lovely stationary; on my daily radio show, I explained to listeners that the word pansy *stands for thought and remembrance; the syndicated newspaper column described how to press and dry pansies...*

And she keeps going! For the media mogul, productivity didn't mean reinventing the wheel to feed her many, many platforms, but taking one core idea and adapting it to each audience. My "pansy" is intimacy and technology, which turned me into a tech culture journalist, a speaker on human connection, and, most recently, the founder of a tech app that facilitated person-to-person intimacy. I'm happy with how my career has gone so far, but it also meant saying "No" to opportunities that would have derailed my journey or diluted my focus.

At the beginning of any new opportunity, the possibilities can seem infinite, and that seemingly exciting wide-open landscape of opportunity can turn into a prison of anxiety and self-doubt. Forget losing productivity; If you get too overwhelmed, you might end up losing yourself.

Learning, developing, and protecting your core is key to being the most productive entrepreneur. You should be able to say it in one short sentence, like an elevator pitch cut in half.

Do you know your core?

3

DEATH BY NETWORKING
You can only talk about an idea so much

I just did something I hadn't done in a while: I went to a networking event. The more time passes, the more I get out of connecting within organic environments and, occasionally, bonding at a small conference. Besides, with now two young kids and a busy business, I don't have much time.

During the cocktail hour, I chatted with an older gentleman, a serial entrepreneur. He asked me if I knew the scene, as he didn't know anyone. I was puzzled, then relieved as I admitted that I hadn't been to a networking event in a while.

We then both realized that we had been too busy *doing* rather than *talking*.

Networking is absolutely important: It grows your brain trust, exposes you to new ideas and gives you a break from the day-to-day grind. But going regularly specifically to networking events has an effect of diminished returns, especially if you are going to them within the same circles. Are you starting to recognize the same people at networking events? Then it's probably time to stop.

One of the great things about parenthood and other external responsibilities is that it forces you not to waste time. Back in Silicon Valley, I would spend hours every week at networking events - as did most people I knew. Mind you, I didn't do the TED Talks, startups, and bigger books until after I left the Silicon Valley networking scene, started a family, and took my time more seriously. I don't think that's a coincidence.

Before I go to an event, networking or otherwise, I ask myself one question:

Is there something more productive I could be doing with this time?

No wonder I, a travel and connecting fanatic, have only gone to only two conferences this year. With all that "extra" time, I wrote a book.

I implore you to ask yourself the same question.

4
WRITE IT DOWN
Ideas go on paper, not on keyboard

Paper is definitely down in popularity, as we are more likely to open up a note application or send a quick email to ourselves than to physically write down something. Even classic journals like Moleskine are going digital.

It's all the more reason to check out NPR's recent interview of two University of California, Los Angeles researchers comparing students' handwritten note taking versus typed out notes. The results were stunning:

"When people type their notes, they have this tendency to try to take verbatim notes and write down as much of the lecture as they can," Mueller tells NPR's Rachel Martin. "The students who were taking longhand notes in our studies were forced to be more selective -- because you can't write as fast as you can type. And that extra

processing of the material that they were doing benefited them."

The scientists found that laptop and written note-takers were equal when it came to facts and figures, but laptop note takers did "significantly worse" when it came to internalizing concepts.

The prevailing theory is this: When you write something by hand, your brain actually has to process the information because it is often not possible to write down every thing being said. Typing, on the other hand, lends itself to speed. You are more likely to try to capture every word rather than jot down the intent.

It is not practical, if impossible to write down everything by hand, but there are some key situations where writing would be more effective than typing:

- Capturing a lecture or presentation
- Preparing for your own lecture or presentation
- Documenting an initial business meeting to set expectations
- Creating a framework for your new business idea

I did a TED Talk on the power of writing our big ideas on little pieces of paper. It doesn't have to be on a little piece of paper, though. It can be on whatever you wish. It is the manual act of writing itself that is valuable.

Today we default to texting something into our smartphone or whipping out the laptop, but we often forget the power of handwriting. Here is why you should consider writing your next thoughts down instead of typing them out.

Filter your thoughts
We go through a filtering process when we write things down. If you're like me,

you can type much faster than you can write--and the additional time and energy required to move your pen means you are more thoughtful in what you capture on the page. It's not limited to words, either: Doing a quick sketch or diagram can sometimes be the key to focusing your thoughts and expressing hard-to-articulate ideas.

Remember what you were thinking
I write everything down on an index card whenever I have a big idea or need to work something out, as cards are compact, portable and efficient. Some of my index card ideas are rubbish, but the ones that are the most valuable eventually get put in a recipe box. (Thankfully, post-TED Talk, they are no longer all over my office.) Now I can access brainstorms or thoughts I had months, even years ago--and they are often strong ideas I would have long forgotten. It's like having a Google for my brain.

Articulate the abstract

Consider it an elevator pitch to yourself. While ideas are broad and encompassing, words are limiting and linear. Use this to your advantage: Find the right language to express your next product or venture. Writing out your thoughts takes them out of your head and forces you to capture them in a cohesive manner without potential distractions or aids like PowerPoint, spellcheck or the World Wide Web. Your scribbles can be both raw in concept and structured in words--a powerful combination.

When is the last time you tried writing down your thoughts, rather than typing things out, to get through an impasse or to work out a strategy?

5
EMPTY YOUR SCHEDULE
Scheduling a blank day will boost your productivity

One of the safest things you can do personally is overcommit yourself. It is also perhaps the worst thing you can do to your business. The security of proving how busy you are and using busyness as a gauge for success will ultimately drop the quality of your interactions, your service and your health. Fighting to be the busiest entrepreneur in the room is an arms race you don't want to win.

My personal cure for overscheduling is to simply schedule a blank day. It doesn't even have to be an entire day. On a regular basis, I will set aside four to 12 hours dedicated to bettering my mind. My phone goes to voicemail, my email is paused, and meetings are pushed to a later date.

These aren't vacation days, but days of self-driven thought, productivity and realignment. Imagine what you could do with a scheduled day of betterment?

- Modify your business plan
- Catch up on must-read materials
- Call previous clients to reconnect

An "unscheduled" day is integral to my business, but it can feel awkward when you first try it. Here's how you can make your own blank day.

Schedule

Yes, you need to schedule your blank day, particularly if you have other people looking at your calendar. Block off the time. Setting it up like a regular meeting trains you to take the blank time seriously. For me, seeing it on my calendar makes me anticipate that day and gives me something to look forward to.

Commit

It is tempting to schedule one or two regular work activities, but even a brief retreat back into your daily grind can take you out of the zone. Instead, commit to the time away just as you would if you were on a Wi-Fi free plane, or sitting in a place with poor cell phone reception, or spending quality time with a loved one. In other words, your office is officially closed for the day.

Maximize

Once you realize your day is open, the possibilities will begin to emerge. Remember, it's not a day of rest, but a day of gathering your mental resources without outside commitments. For me, my blank days are when I finish books, go for thoughtful walks and catch up with dormant clients. They are days to restrategize, retool and recommit. It is me sharpening my axe so I can be a more effective warrior.

6
WHEN TO LET IT GO
Knowing when to stop working is just as important

Except for death and parenting, few things inspire as many quotations and axioms as entrepreneurship. They usually encourage us to keep going: "Fight another day," "It is darkest before the dawn," "Failure just eliminates another bad option," and so on.

Other people need encouragement to keep going. Entrepreneurs, though, need encouragement to *stop*. We're too motivated as it is. Anyone who enters the odds-adverse entrepreneurial world has to be, on some level, an optimist. If anything, we push when we should be still and we goad when we should be receptive. In fact, as discussed in the original THE BITE-SIZED ENTREPRENEUR, our restlessness can destroy something that is already on its way to success.

In my experience, there are three great reasons not to make any more moves on an opportunity:

The launch date/commitment time is already here

Legend has it that Alex Haley's publisher had to send a representative to the author's house to literally pull the *Roots* manuscript out of his hands. As this famed African saga was inspired by Haley's family tree, the author could have kept adding more and more details. But it was too late.

You have a commitment to excellence, but you have a bigger commitment to serve your audience. A great product or service is useless if it never ships.

You did everything you could

Sometimes, there are flaws, challenges, or gaps in what we are presenting, but there is absolutely nothing we can do about it. I experience this regularly in the journalism world, where external factors like page layout, the publication date, and budgetary constraints can severely affect the end result. It is a lesson in doing the best you can… and letting go.

It is in someone else's hands
The roughest part of entrepreneurship, at least for me, isn't the ideation/creation phase, nor the so-called crunch time before launching a product, but the gap where you wait for someone else's response. It could be the audience after a launch, or a partner after you made a big decision, or even a vendor once an important request was submitted. You know the result is important, but there is nothing more for you to do.

Everyone has a method of calming his or her inner control freak. My regular process is talking out loud through the various scenarios and having a plan A, B, and C in place. For me, having my next chess moves planned calms things down. And, once feedback is given, I'll know exactly what move I should start executing.

7
WALK IT OUT
Get on your feet to recharge your productivity

It has been a turbulent summer of sorts for many of us, with the political unrest, stock market volatility and crazy, dangerous weather. I've been dealing with my own unique stress, reflecting on my anniversary escaping Hurricane Katrina, selling my popular app Cuddlr, and transitioning out of a 3 a.m. daily work routine.

So, one day recently, I just got up from my computer, left the house and started walking. Probably about four miles that day.

I've always loved walking, particularly when I lived in the heart of San Francisco, where it would be a rare day when I didn't walk to tech functions throughout the evening (the city is seven by seven miles, so walking everywhere isn't an unrealistic accomplishment). I then moved to Southern California in which most cities, unlike New York, Chicago and D.C., aren't conducive to walking everywhere. I also started a family, and those hours spent walking-or hours spent doing anything-seemed as impractical as they seemed wasteful. But now I'm taking the time to walk, whether it be in the morning or in the night, as I'm realizing it is how I clear my mind and how I process my day. It has been like a meditation, though many of us who do walk regularly may not even realize the positive impact it has on our mental balance.

Walking for clarity isn't a revolutionary idea. According to *The Last Great Walk* author Wayne Curtis, the health benefits of regular walking came into view about a century ago-particularly when it came to keeping ourselves young.

What is new is that entrepreneurs are actually starting to value it. Consultant Nilofer Merchant has a short, excellent TED talk on why business people should take walking seriously. As we spend more time on tech and less time taking care of ourselves, I tend to agree.

Here's how you can incorporate walking into your daily entrepreneurial life.

Do walking meetings
Walking can be an excellent time to take conference calls, especially those that have you mostly on mute. If you are fortunate enough to work near your colleagues, take them with you on a brief jaunt. It may help you work out knotty ideas or even ease the tension of a particularly sensitive conversation-Steve Jobs famously had his most important discussions on his feet.

Get smart
It is also a great opportunity to listen to business books or, on the free side, to

podcasts. I now listen to Startup, Will Lucas' Of10, and other favorite entrepreneurial podcasts almost exclusively during my walks. It not only makes the time more valuable, but it assuages any guilt that I'm out of the office.

Keep it brief

A walk doesn't have to be an extreme, epic journey-it could be walking to a farther coffee shop for your morning drink or spending an extra 10 minutes taking the long way to lunch. You can look at the additional time as a brief reprieve from the constant device buzz.

Track your walks

If you're into measurable results, consider utilizing a wearable, whether it be a FitBit or Apple Watch, or an old-school pedometer. The ability to see how many steps or miles you've walked can help encourage you to keep going and, perhaps, walk even further the next time you go out.

8

STOP MEASURING TIME
Never mistake time for commitment

Time is often how we measure our commitment to an idea. Someone who put in 20 years developing something successful is looked at as persistent, visionary, and patient. On the other hand, calling someone an "overnight success" is usually a backhanded complement, as it shows a person who potentially got lucky or stumbled upon a brilliant idea. The quick ride to success is looked at with both admiration and envy. They didn't earn their stripes.

The one important thing time does not measure is commitment. Side hustlers, folks that take time outside of their main gig to take their passion seriously, can easily be more committed than full-timers. Can you imagine taking time away from your rest, your leisure, and your life outside of your full-time job to make your dream a reality? Perhaps you can. Perhaps you are doing that right now.

Time spent does not indicate passion nor focus, hence it not equating commitment. Social scientists are now poking holes in the 10,000 hours theory made popular in Malcolm Gladwell's influential *Outliers*. Gladwell argued that mastery of a particular skill happens when someone puts in 10,000 hours of study and practice, citing Bill Gates, The Beatles, and other modern icons. The rub, though, is that we don't know how *focused* people were during those 10,000 hours. Picture Salvador Dali spending countless days doing still life and never progressing into the abstract, disturbing art for which he is known. He was fully present during those proverbial 10,000 hours, and that gave him the vision to create beyond the literal bread and baskets that he painted early in his career. Again, time does not equate *quality time*.

Instead, as Dali went abstract, The

Beatles went psychedelic, and Gates went visionary, you should measure your productivity by your evolution. Your growth could be a radical, public departure. Your growth could be a subtle shift inside. It doesn't matter.

As spiritual writer Pema Chodron puts it, "In order to go deeper, there has to be a wholehearted commitment. You begin the warrior's journey when you choose one path and stick to it. Then you let it put you through your changes."

Focus on transformation based on what you are doing, not on the time you spend doing it.

II: DOING

"The professional does not wait for inspiration; he acts in anticipation of it."

-Steven Pressfield, *Turning Pro*

9

DO LESS WITH MORE IMPACT
Being productive every day is a fool's errand

If busyness is our number one obsession today, then constant productivity is a close second. I'm part of the problem: I not only analyze how some of the most interesting leaders stay focused, but I am obsessed with being productive myself. I had my Masters by my very early 20's and wrote 18 books in the past decade. I've got my own issues.

So perhaps you'll listen when I say this: *You are not meant to be productive all the time.* We seem to think that there is some magic formula that turns our mushy, balanced-oriented human brains into tough, binary computers. There is not.

The best way to be productive is to let yourself be less productive.

Take it one goal at a time

It's no coincidence that some of the most recognized entrepreneurs ruthlessly focus on one thing at a time. Focusing on multiple things doesn't make us get more done, but simply makes us less productive in several areas.

Focus in intervals

I call them palate cleansers, after the refresher you eat or drink between meal courses. The idea is to focus on something for a short, intense period of time, then to give yourself a break.

Break early, break often

Walking, quiet time, blank days, Internet unplugging, and other disconnections do marvelous things to your productivity because your brain will continue to problem solve while you take in the quiet.

If you really want to get amazing things done, then trade in busyness for productivity. And that happens best in intense cycles, not in breathless marathons.

10

THE NECESSARY THING
Sometimes you can only do one thing well

When I was burning the candle in the middle (well beyond burning it at both ends) and considering giving up, one of my mentors, Rosemary Taylor, gave me a simple directive.

"Chop wood, carry water."

In other words, sometimes the best thing you can do is do the routine, the necessary thing, that needs to be done at the moment, and concentrate on absolutely nothing else. Focus on the first thing, the necessary thing, and then go to the next thing on the list.

That's it. And that is enough for today.

11

ALTERNATE TASKS

Palate cleansers can refresh your focus and productivity

As an entrepreneur, I tend to run hot and cold. I'm burning the midnight oil for weeks, then I have several days where my intensity and, seemingly, my passion seems to dissipate. Unfortunately, that means wasting excess energy when all the work is done and potentially not being as thorough as possible when the energy is low. I know the extreme decision-making trap firsthand.

One practice that helps immensely is palate cleansing. You are taking something to wash away the previous experience to make way for the next one. Mint, bread, and even plain old water are popular palate cleansers, but what if you applied it to your daily actions? Here's food for thought.

Focus on something else

In food, a palate cleanser is usually a light drink or snack that makes your senses focus on something else. It serves as a bridge between two courses. The courses themselves are usually strong or intense. The palate cleanser serves as a break between two extreme experiences, helping you digest the former and get prepared for the latter.

The irony is delicious, here: The more focus you want, the more you need to step away.

Make time to rebuild your focus

I love deep diving into work, but intensity, by its very nature, is in limited quantity. In fact, researchers estimate that you can only hold your complete attention onto something for a couple of hours. (It's the reason why public speakers follow the adage, "Say what you're going to tell them, tell them what you're going to tell them, and then tell them what you just told them.")

It is the reason why it doesn't make much sense to do a 20-hour day with little or no breaks: Your productivity will drop, sooner rather than later, and you may actually be wasting time rather than maximizing it. The 25-minute Pomodoro Technique is the epitome of short focus, but even a 15-minute break every hour or two would be much more efficient than creating a marathon day.

Give room for thought
Why do palate cleansers make you more productive? While you may have checked out, your brain is still focused on the previous project and creating smarter strategies for you to use when you start again. As I recently talked about, resting may be our most powerful entrepreneurial tool. People in traditional lines of work usually can't build their own schedule from scratch! It is a perk that may have gotten us into entrepreneurship, but something we tend to forget after we become entrepreneurs.

A short, daily meditation is my palate cleanser, as is going for a walk and, whenever possible, taking a brief nap. Yours may be checking social media, doing a quick exercise or reaching out to a colleague for a quick chat. We all should find ways to take our ostrich-like heads out of the sand.

12

OVEREXTENDING YOURSELF
Burning out doesn't have to happen

It is remarkably easy to do too much, particularly when you love what you do. Does work not feel like work? You may be fortunate enough to be in that situation, but that also means you are less likely to know when you are tilting towards burnout, physically in need of rest, or pushing yourself too hard. Entrepreneurs may have more passion around their career than most, so we are more susceptible to losing ourselves in the excitement of work.

Self-care is a part of taking care of our business, because if we break down, then our business will break down, too. Here are some solid ways to help stave off overextension.

Wait to commit
We feel pressure to say "Yes" to opportunities right away because we're

afraid of missing the boat or, worse, our measured response will scare away the person who's offering the opportunity itself. I've found that some opportunities are fleeting, but the number is nowhere near the number of opportunities that we think are fleeting. In other words, when it comes to determining the rarity of an opportunity, we tend to sit on the paranoid side. Unfortunately, that means we are more likely to say "Yes" to things even when we don't have the resources to take them on. And... suddenly we're overextended.

Instead, try taking a moment to consider letting go of the opportunity being offered. It could be five minutes, it could be an entire evening. Give yourself as much space as can be allotted. You may be surprised at the new considerations that suddenly pop up, ideas that would not have otherwise crossed your mind until, perhaps, it was too late.

Check your gut

Some opportunities can feel particularly rare because they are actually a little too ideal. Fortunately, our gut can give us the warning that we should look deeper. For myself, I may get a feeling that someone is holding back information or that the deal may end up in a different place than intended. It is often right, but the most important part to understand is that your gut isn't specific - it just realizes when something feels off with a situation. And it very well may be telling you that a new opportunity will be too much of a strain on your resources.

Ask a colleague

Sometimes the one to help you stay in check is a trusted confidant. If you have your brain trust in order, then you already have people around you who know your goals, your intentions and your weaknesses. An objective party can warn you when you are veering off your path or potentially falling prey to one of your blind spots.

Look back a year from now

One of the best ways to prevent overextending yourself is to envision how you'd like to spend your time, energy, and focus a year from now. What will you be doing? How will you be doing it? What seeds do you need to plant to get there?

There are few reality checks bigger than realizing the work you are doing now won't get you to where you want to be. No one intends to be unproductive towards his or her dreams. It's just that, when we overextend ourselves, we are too overcommitted and scattered to prioritize the things that will move us closer to our goal over the busy work we're already doing. Think about where you want to go and plan on saying "No" to plans that don't move you forward. "No" should be your default, and seemingly nonessential opportunities should have to be important enough to convince you otherwise.

13
MASTERING TIME
How you can maximize your schedule

Time management master Laura Vanderkam has written several books, including the best-seller *168 Hours*, on how even the most in-demand leaders maintain incredible productivity. She and I agree that the most precious resource you have isn't money, but time.

I got a chance to connect with Vanderkam when she spoke at the recent American Society of Journalists and Authors conference. She shared three master tips to strong time management.

Write down how you spend your time
Create a time journal, not unlike people concerned with their eating habits create a food journal. How can you maximize your time if you aren't sure how you're really spending it?

Vanderkam admitted that she thought she worked 60 hours a week but, after keeping a time journal for several months, realized it was closer to 40 hours a week. By keeping a journal, you can squeeze out the inefficiencies and better understand why you may not feel as productive as you think you should be.

Do a (time) portfolio review

Do a portfolio review of how you spend your time, just like you would for stock performance. In this case, however, you are looking at the allocation of your time assets. Are you spending 10 percent of your time sending and tracking invoicing? Then we're talking five to six weeks out of every year.

Vanderkam found that virtual assistants, interns and smart software can help immensely - and the financial outlay pales compared to the time you save. How else could you be growing your business with the proverbial 10 percent of your year you'd get back?

Done is better than perfect
The ultimate time suck is perfection. Spending too much time perfecting a product or service not only can hurt your business, but it can create opportunity cost for the other great, new things you could be working on.

Vanderkam highly recommends this: "Let it go. Done is better than perfect." Think about the last time you spent an inordinate amount of time for an incremental improvement on a completed project. Now imagine all the other things you could have been doing with that time. At a certain point, spending more time on something will provide significantly diminished returns. Being honest about when you reach that point is perhaps the toughest, most important skill in great time management.

14

PUT THE COFFEE DOWN
Drinking coffee at the wrong time will hurt your day

Unlike many entrepreneurs, I didn't drink coffee through school, nor in young adulthood, and it didn't keep me going during business all nighters and crunch times (adrenaline did that). No, I didn't fall in love with coffee until well into my grown-up life when I began appreciating its bitter, robust flavor.

Thankfully, it was just before taking on a 3 a.m. schedule, but the energy boost has always been a perk, not a reason.

Culturally we usually have coffee first thing in the morning, but I realized that it was much more powerful and effective when I had it later in the day-- like 11 a.m. The days went smoother and I focused better. Now science is backing it up, though there are many reasons to hold off on that first cup of java.

Your body doesn't need coffee early
Your body begins pumping cortisol when you wake up in the morning, kind of like a smelling salt to help you rise and shine. The boost happens between 8 a.m. – 9 a.m., followed by other boosts midday and in late afternoon. Drinking coffee first thing in the morning is like adding lighter fluid to an already-growing fire: You quickly burn extra bright, and you burn out just as fast.

However, drinking a cup between 9:30 a.m. to 11:30 a.m. provides an energy bridge between your early cortisol rises. Around 11 a.m. is my sweet spot. It is also important to put the science in context: 8 a.m. was once the perfect time for me to have coffee, but that was when I was waking up at 3:15 a.m., so 8 a.m. was my midday cup.

Coffee can mask your true entrepreneurial feelings

For a caffeine-sensitive person like myself, coffee can make one feel like everything is coming together: You're being super productive, ideas are coming easily, and business is going in the right direction! All the above may or may not be true, but I want to feel that way because of the passion for my business or the rewards of a hard-earned strategy, not because a bean is making me feel brilliant.

As a stimulant, coffee can make us excited about awful ideas, abrasive about our opinions and unable to settle down (or perhaps that's just me!). It can bring out the opposite skills we need to be the best entrepreneur we can be. The potential issue is compounded when we drink it when our bodies are already revving up for the day. Overdoing the coffee first thing in the morning can have us starting the day making bad decisions.

It breaks up your day

The 3 p.m. drag is real, particularly after a heavy lunch, but late morning is often when we really begin to slow down from the rush. The average work day starts with a 6 a.m. jolt of the alarm, the body shock of shower water, the dash for the train or car, the social stimulation of people or traffic and the productivity burst with the intent of catching up or getting things done early in the day. In other words, you're running a sprint until lunch is on the horizon. No wonder we slow down at lunch and need a nap around 2ish.

The 11 a.m. coffee creates a natural break in the day--the transition from sunrise to sunset. On more mellow days, I'll replace my late morning coffee with a strong tea or fruit-infused water. When I do coffee, though, I take it a step further and make it a physical transition by making my coffee by hand with a French press. It takes about five minutes, grinding the beans, pouring in the hot water and pushing down the stopper. For me, it is like a meditation on what I already got done today and what I will get done later. It is a thoughtful pause.

15
KNOW YOUR PRIME TIME
Everyone peaks at different moments

When I was young, my golden hours were from 1 o'clock until dawn. It was something about the silence of the night, the gap between bedtime and rise, that turned me alive. I'd have all kinds of ideas. My writing would flow. An optimistic glaze would cover my world. It wasn't until I couldn't stay up all night (hello, family) that I realized how much my creativity was fueled by certain rituals - and, in this case, certain schedules.

I recently heard the term "golden hours" from People Matters founder Jodi Wehling. I take it as more than just your most productive time of the day. No, it's when you are at your peak in creativity, vision and inspiration - even without a cup of coffee. Here Wehling describes them:

Pay attention over the next week and identify when your best work hours are.

Then guard them with your life. Block the time and mark it as "busy". Resist the temptation to book this time for a meeting.

This is your time. It is worth twice as much as other times in terms of what you can get accomplished.

As a leader, it is terribly easy to let outside forces dictate your schedule. If you get more successful, then defending your own needs becomes harder, not easier.

There are two great, actionable ways to make your golden hours work:

Say no

Nope. Uhn-uh. Can't right now. I recently talked about three smart, strategic ways to say no and save your relationships. Denying people access to you 24/7 is the only way you can preserve your productivity.

Create a blank day

Block off an entire day and make no meetings, phone calls or messaging available. Not only will it give you the space to think, which we rarely create, but it also will give a glimpse into when your golden hours actually are. Undisturbed, I'm productive mid morning, mid afternoon and late evenings, which is much different than when I started my career or even during my early morning rituals a couple years ago. Having a blank day will show you your natural productivity patterns *at this moment*.

Save your energy

Bracket your golden hours with less intensive activities. For instance, if I have meetings or interviews, I place them before or after my most productive moments. It is a great way to preserve your outside work needs and protect your golden hours.

When are your golden hours?

16
THE HARDEST 1%
The last step is by far the most dangerous

I launched my first app, So Quotable, after many years of development, with the app's programmer abandoning the project at the last minute, and four months of learning Apple programming language in the wee hours while taking care of my first son. It was brutal. It launched as a workable, functional product just in time for my first TED talk. I showed it with a mixture of pride and shame, as I could quite see the bubble gum and duct tape that kept it together. I knew it inside and out, so I knew all of its flaws.

Shortly after launch, I showed it with trepidation to a professional, successful programmer who knew my journey. He paused wordlessly for a moment, then gave this big smile.

"I'm impressed!"

"Ha! It's pretty damn rough. What are you impressed by?"

"You shipped."

He knew, I knew, and now you know a secret: You will never want to ship. What you create will never be good enough for the public. If you are doing your job right, then you can name at least five things you would change about the thing you are about to give the world. If you aren't insecure about your next big reveal, then you are either lazy or lying.

Artists don't create. Artists ship. Wrote something that you never show to another soul? You just made a diary entry, not a novel. Make a brilliant product that is stuck in almost done? You just created an amazing demo, not something people can actually use. At this point, your influence will be nil. To paraphrase motivational speaker Steve Harvey, you'll be safe, but you'll never soar.

Off the top of my head, I know several talented people who thrive in the 99% zone: brilliant artists, founders, and creatives – nay, *aspiring* artists, founders, and creatives – who charge like a wrecking ball towards their goals. And then, just as the final piece comes into place, they stop. I bring this up not from a place of judgment, but just to show you how deadly that final 1% can be for anyone creative. The dream of what could be is a strong, seductive opiate compared to the cold reality of your realized idea, filled with bumps and bruises and compromises and constraints, exposed to the elements of criticism and judgment.

It's never starting an idea that shows you are serious about your commitment. It is finishing an idea.

III: RENEWING

"With affluence and power come escalating expectations, and as our level of wealth and comforts keeps increasing, the sense of well-being we hoped to achieve keeps receding into the distance."

- Mihaly Csikszentmihalyi, Flow

17

OPTING OUT

Always know why you are doing what you are doing

Why are you at work today? I don't mean your paycheck work, but your so-called passionate work. For us, work could mean pushing out another product, going to a networking event, or updating your website. Why are you doing it right now? Why are you compelled to produce, to move... to show up?

The question is not as banal as it seems. Mainstream musicians come out with a new album every 18 months, often not because they are inspired like clockwork, but because they (and/or their publishers) are afraid the public will forget their name. Authors churn out books to keep themselves known, too, and even if they currently have a best-seller, they will want to have another one coming as the current one takes its' inevitable fall off the charts. Entrepreneurs fight for success, get that success, and then immediately chase after the next success as they don't want to be viewed as a one-hit wonder.

I can relate to two out of three of these things (hint: I don't play any instruments).

What all three of these examples, and countless other similar scenarios, have in common is fear. We are afraid of losing our place in the world. If we stop, then we will be replaced with a newer, smarter model. We must feed the beast.

It may be the most widely used performance hack. It is also the most short sighted.

It's like performing with a gun to your head: Sure, it gets you motivated to be productive, but at a certain point your body, mind, or soul will give out and you will have to stop, no matter the consequences. That's called burnout. It's called being productive the wrong way.

Instead, you have to listen to, understand by, and give respect to your natural cycle. You will not be productive all the time. You are not meant to be productive all the time. In fact, you are best when you are not productive all the time, as less productive periods give you the opportunity to think, to strategize, and to optimize your energy for the next sprint.

If you want to understand why we often don't respect our own productive cycles, then you have to look at how we view others. As creatives – and entrepreneurs, no matter the ilk, are creatives, too – we face a tremendous amount of pressure to perform. You came up with a brilliant melody? Come up with another one. Can we get another game-changing novel? When are you going to get another startup idea that will shift business forever? We are all guilty of having these expectations, explicitly or implicitly, on the creatives we admire the most. It is why we get desperate, angry, or dismissive at the Salingers of the world: People who produce based on some personal schedule, not on some worldly expectation.

Vulture's Rembert Browne articulated the psychosis well in an article about Andre 3000, Frank Ocean, and other mainstream performers who produce seemingly on their own time:

High quality multi-talents with both infrequent outputs and low profiles make us uncomfortable. We love them, but we're jealous of them, and, possibly, deep down we hate them, because they're doing what we all want to do: Opt out. The way they've decided to live reminds us of how wrong we're all doing it. When people go against the grain of the system, it's a reminder that we're the robots — and the weirdos are the actual humans.

The lessons here are many. First, productivity comes in two forms: Productivity for the public approval and productivity for your passion. It's possible to discover transformative ideas and map out brilliant strategies *without anyone else knowing and with no public proof.* It's OK.

Second, if you produce all the time, then it is easy to lose your voice for the sound of the crowd. The outside voices could be your customers, your family, or your backers. Remember, the people have invested in *your* voice, not the other way around.

No one is going to tell you when it is time to put the tools away and sit down for a second. Only you know when that moment is. And you absolutely always know when that moment is. You just need to be brave enough to listen.

18
LOOKING FOR A CRISIS
Avoid making things up to feel productive

If you are like me, then you get excitement from making difficult situations manageable and impossible scenarios work. Business, and startups specifically, strive on people disrupting monolithic systems and solving long-term problems.

The issue is that the very same bug that gets under our skin to fix things can also make us addicted to the rush of chaos. VC Mark Suster calls it "urgency addiction" and defines it well better than I can:

People with the "urgency addition" thrive on the pressure. We rise to the occasion as it stirs our creative juices. There is something about the adrenaline rush of being under time pressure that excites us and teases out our creativity. We get away with having the urgency addiction because we perform well under pressure. Not everybody does.

The problem, Suster says, is that there a lot of things that are urgent, but few that are important. As he mentions, productivity guru Stephen Covey discussed the idea many years ago in the seminal book *First Things First.*

I have sympathy for Suster and his type of urgency addiction, but I believe it goes a bit deeper than that.

There are two types of urgency addition: personality and environmental.

Suster's great post breaks down what it's like for someone who has a personality leaning towards urgency. As he says, everything is a crisis, and rushing to get things done makes him feel accomplished. More worrisome, he gets a great adrenaline rush from when he finishes things, saving himself from ruin just in the nick of time.

My urgency addiction, however, is different. Throw me on a proverbial desert island and I will be as calm as the breeze. Put me around other people, though, and it can be terribly easy to absorb their attitude - particularly if they are in crisis mode. I'd call this an environmental urgency addiction.

A good personal example for me would be my young family. If you have kids, then you know that minor things to adults are big, imposing things to little ones, which means meltdowns, tears and frustrations. Transpose that energy into a startup (yes, there is a direct parallel between the two experiences) and you can see how a chaotic environment can put me into urgency mode over things that are relatively minor. You are orbiting the giant hairball, as the late Gordon MacKenzie put it, and trying not to get caught in it.

Whether you are a personal or environmental urgency junkie, there are a few survival tactics to keep your head together.

- Remind yourself that it isn't a crisis
- Ask yourself if it will matter 5 minutes, 5 months or 5 years from now
- Forgive yourself for going there

In *The War of Art*, Steven Pressfield found that creatives were more susceptible to "creating soap opera in our lives". However, unlike the amateur, "The working artist will not tolerate trouble in her life because she knows trouble prevents her from doing her work." We need the excitement and the adventure, but it is much easier to make personal drama than it is for us to sit down, shut up, and put that passion into our art.

Think about all the things that feel like a crisis in your life right now, and then how many are real, absolute crisis that have no chance of being resolved on their own. If you channeled that excess anxiety over imagined crisis into your work, then how productive would you be   today?

19
LESS, BETTER EMAIL
Do less emails, more action

Inbox Zero is a great, wonderful goal, where you have no emails sitting in your mailbox. It is also fairly unrealistic for an entrepreneur. How often do you have every deal, relationship and invoice wrapped up like so many loose threads tied into a neat bow? I actually achieved it once recently, and keeping it is a daily battle.

Clearing our inbox may be a Sisyphean affair, but we're ignoring another part of the problem: The length of the messages we get. The longer the email, the longer it often takes to get to the actual action item. And as much as fellow communication specialists decry the shortening of our language in texts, emojis, and, well, Slack, we still manage to write emails the length of newspaper articles.

Can't we just get to the point? Evidently not.

Fast Company's Liz Funk recently ran a good (and short!) piece on the rules to briefer stronger emails. It's worth reading in whole, but I particularly like her best rule:

"2. Never send an email that's more than five sentences long"

That's right. How much more effective would your messaging be if you got straight to the point? It's not a matter of being curt or brisk, but circumventing all the unnecessary fluff that goes into your email discussions.

Sticking to five sentences means you can't acquiesce when it comes to an "ask", nor can you hide in "maybes" when you actually mean "no". Instead, you are forced to be clear, succinct and respectful of everyone's time - including your own.

All of Funk's top three rules are worth considering, too:

1. Take the number of words you think your email should be, cut that number in half, and that's what your word count should be.

2. Never send an email that's more than five sentences long.

3. Put the most important information first.

I'd add a few more rules myself:

4. Consider email part of a bigger conversation, not the whole conversation, so it isn't necessary to put every single detail in one note.

5. Assume the reader does not have much time to pore over your email.

6. If an email is becoming abnormally lengthy, then perhaps email is not the right medium.

Most of all, I appreciate Funk's the simple summary of why you should care:

For solopreneurs, freelancers, and sales professionals who make their living pitching, having a perfectly crafted, short email introduction can drastically increase your success rate. For those making an ask via email, a message that is brief and adds value is more likely to receive a response. For everyone else, sending shorter emails doesn't always take less time, but it does stack the odds in your favor for whatever you aim to accomplish.

Isn't that enough to take the five-sentence challenge? I know it is for me.

20
CREATE "ME" TIME
Even ambitious entrepreneurs can create space for themselves

Entrepreneurship isn't conducive to balanced health, balanced relationships or, really, balanced anything. The rub is that the very vacation, break, or me-time you are postponing could give you the insight you need to move your business forward. We expect to be geniuses at business, but don't give ourselves time to recharge our brains.

I get it: My daily life has been raising my young family, writing and public speaking, and, most recently, leading my startup to acquisition. Here are three ways I keep myself together.

Meditate
Perhaps you, like I once did, think of monk-filled temples or planning to learn it during a trip to the mountains. I view it now as just taking a moment to be

fully present in your life: No multitasking, no planning, and no distractions. I rarely get silence, so I will carve out a time daily to sit cross-legged, close my eyes, and breathe in and out. I just do it for a few minutes a day, usually every day. And, as my Buddhist friend A. Raymond Johnson once shared with me, even riding a bike or washing the dishes can be turned into a meditative activity. It is about stopping, fully taking in your life and enjoying it.

Do one selfish thing

It is crucial to do something daily that has absolutely nothing to do with anyone or anything else. It means it won't grow your business, help your family, or improve your money. If you can carve out time to juggle your business, your personal relationships and other commitments, you can make 10 minutes to do something fun just for you. For me, as a music fan, it might mean taking a random moment in the day to listen to John Coltrane uninterrupted. It is surprisingly refreshing.

Have downtime

As entrepreneurs, we often try to kill two birds with one stone by incorporating our research or work into our downtime: Reading a business book or watching a TED Talk on our business area. I argue that this isn't really downtime, but light work. To mean, downtime means doing something not related to your work at all: It may mean watching a viral video to see what the talk is about, going on a walk in your neighborhood, or spending a few minutes catching up with an old friend.

21

THE WHISKEY METHOD
Look back to go forward

Forgetting the past will not make you more productive. It is a common misconception. Smart planning, excellent ideas, and impressive vision will not help you if you don't possess two traits: Confidence and gratitude. Both reside in your history.

The past reminds you of what you have overcome, which gives you confidence to move forward, and it shows you what you have accomplished, which gives you gratitude for the current moment.

Confidence can be relatively easy to find, but gratitude is a rather slippery one. The most productive people have their own wise method of finding it: *The 4-Hour Work Week* author Tim Ferriss writes briefly in a gratitude journal every morning and night, while media mogul Oprah Winfrey meditates often.

I regularly meditate and occasionally journal, too, but my most effective process is reminding myself where I was a year, five years, or even ten years ago.

I call it the Whiskey Method.

A few years back, the popular scotch whiskey Johnny Walker had a wonderful ad campaign. They would take a popular icon or even an upstart entrepreneur and show their timeline to their modern success. As a made-up example, "1966 Backup Guitarist, 1967 Debut Album, 1969 Rock Legend" would be for Jimi Hendrix. It would end with a simple motto: "Keep walking".

The problem is that we tend to lionize people, particularly ourselves, *after* they've made it. We often don't define what "making it" means, nor do we celebrate the many, many victories it takes to even get there. We don't respect the journey. And, as writers more thoughtful than I have said, you can't expect to be given more if you don't appreciate what you already have. Why would your so-called muse deliver more creativity and insight when you didn't give her props for helping you in the past? The Whiskey Method is that gratitude.

Here is mine:
- 2005 Published First Book
- 2010 Published First Best-seller
- 2013 Started First Startup
- 2014 Did First TED Talk
- 2015 Sold Second Startup

It is both inspiring and humbling to me that I just began writing books about a decade ago, and you are now reading my 18th one. It is even more beautiful that I started my entrepreneurial journey only three years ago, yet have had enough adventures to share with others. I immediately feel like forgiving myself for the mistakes I've made this month, this week, or even this day.

The frustrations, setback, and challenges in my day-to-day grind begin to fall away, as I realize not that much time has passed. I am still a student. And now, as I realize how quickly I've transformed as a person, I start to respect the progress I make today – and that means I'll be more productive than I would have been otherwise.

22

SILENCE IS GOLDEN

Periodically shut up to make progress

It's always more comfortable to take action. It is the negotiator who can't handle the uncomfortable lull in the conversation, the artist who keeps fiddling with her finished work or the child who has to do what he was just told not to do. The absence of something is always more frightening than having undesired results from our actions.

If we embraced silence as part of the natural ebb and flow of our lives, then we would be stronger, smarter, and savvier when it is actually time to take action. Meditation, yoga and other practices can help get your mind into a clearer space.
You can also just stop talking.

A recent Duke University study found that quiet actually improves memory and awareness, per *Nautilus Magazine*:

Kirste found that two hours of silence per day prompted cell development in the hippocampus, the brain region related to the formation of memory, involving the senses. This was deeply puzzling: The total absence of input was having a more pronounced effect than any sort of input tested.

Here's how Kirste made sense of the results. She knew that "environmental enrichment," like the introduction of toys or fellow mice, encouraged the development of neurons because they challenged the brains of mice. Perhaps the total absence of sound may have been so artificial, she reasoned--so alarming, even--that it prompted a higher level of sensitivity or alertness in the mice.

Like taking a short nap or planning a blank day, creating quiet time is a conscious act towards productivity disguised as a leisure activity. We schedule power meetings, brainstorms, hackathons, and vacations. Why aren't we scheduling silence? It is worth blocking off a daily hour of quiet - not inactivity, but silence - and seeing how it changes your productivity.

23

BULLETPROOF

The more you know yourself, the more space you have to be productive

Pressure to be productive can actually stress us out to the point where we are no longer potent, and it usually comes from two places: internal and external. The internal pressure reminds you that there is a particular, often idealized goal you planned to reach and you will absolutely not reach it if you do not hit a certain level of productivity. The external pressure tells you that other people will judge you or, worse, stop you from reaching the goal if you aren't being productive fast enough.

The internal pressure can be relieved by setting realistic milestones, creating limitations to encourage focus, and maintaining your self-care. The external pressure is much more nefarious. It is the competitor that you know now, or perhaps the unknown competitor in the near future that can snuff you out at any time. It is the loved one that, whether he said anything or not, you know is just waiting for you to fail so he can be proven right. It is the loyal customers who you think will be disappointed if you do not deliver as quickly as you would like. It is the invisible "they". And, to use a popular sports saying, "They cannot be stopped, only contained."

Containing the external pressure can be done in one simple way: Understand what you are not. By knowing what you are not, you have little to worry about with other people derailing or duplicating your success. A good example is the ride-sharing services Lyft and Uber. On paper, they sound like similar companies, both employing everyday drivers to turn their own vehicles into ad hoc taxis. The identities couldn't be more different, though: Uber pushes the remote, cool personal limo feel, as it originally only utilized black cars, while Lyft represents the fun, collegiate experience, with its cars initially having big pink moustaches stuck on their bumpers. Talk about branding! I know many creatives that hate the word "branding", but that's what you are doing when you say you only work with small organizations, or your boutique caters to the working class, or your startup was created for hungry millennials, and so on. It is what separates *you* from *them*. And separating yourself is a hell of a lot easier when it comes from your own identity, as you don't have to work so hard to be authentic. I heard Uber co-founder Travis Kalanick speak at TED and there is no way you could see him and believe he created Lyft. The Uber brand is a representation of him, through and through. You nor I could recreate Uber, even with a billion dollars. Uber belongs only to Travis. People can compete, but they cannot replicate.

Identifying what you are not, and therefore quieting the external pressure, is important for two reasons. First, putting the focus on proving something to the outside world is a ridiculous task: If you are doing anything worthwhile, then there will be critics, and those critics will never be silenced. It is a waste of precious time. Second, worrying about the external pressure will take you out of your own natural productive cycle. Get in the wrong headspace and you could be shipping products to please the public when your work actually needed more time to gestate, or taking on more duties to hush critics when you should be better managing your tasks at hand. Again, you have an instinct for when you should be pursuing, when you should be doing, and when you should be renewing. Not having a rock-solid identity could have you dramatically trying to force productivity based on the fickle public.

Master marketer Seth Godin explains it further:

"At some point, you need to decide who you are. You need to understand the scale of what you built. You need to decide what the brand is when people hire you and when they engage with you… [and] we can't jump to the next thing instantly nor can we complain that picking one scale keeps us from doing the other thing. We have to embrace it. The fact is that it helps us that we have a sinecure, that we have a niche, that we have a thing that we do, 'cuz then, when other people want to be in our space just for kicks, they can't! They are not us at our scale with our contribution to make."

The more you clarify what you are not, the more bulletproof you become. Then you can take your time, follow your own productivity cycle, and push away worries about being replaced – because you can't be.

24

SHADOWBOXING

Fact: Most of your fears will not come to pass

Entrepreneurship is all about anticipation. You have to know what the market wants before you deliver or, when it comes to the financial end, what the markets will bear before you price your product. You have to guess what your competition is going to do when you launch your service. You have to be ready for when your idea goes viral because, as argued in THE BITE-SIZED ENTREPRENEUR, you have to prepare for success as much as you do for failure.

And why, again, are we more prone to anxiety and sleepless nights? Honestly, it could be a chicken and egg paradox, as entrepreneurial personalities tend to be focused on the future anyway.

The question is, what do you do with all that nervousness about tomorrow?

Nothing.

Recognize it, sit with it, accept it, and let it leave.

The spiritual writer Pema Chodron has a great analogy for us. It is unedited and shown at length for full effect:

There's a Zen story in which a man is enjoying himself on a river at dusk. He sees another boat coming down the river toward him. At first it seems so nice to him that someone else is also enjoying the river on a nice summer evening. Then he realized that the boat is coming right toward him, faster and faster. He begins to yell, "Hey, hey, watch out! For Pete's sake, turn aside!" But the boat just comes right at him, faster and faster. By this time he's standing up in his boat, screaming and shaking his fist, and then the boat smashes right into him. He sees that it's an empty boat.

I laughed out loud when I first read this

story more than a decade ago. I laughed again when I stumbled upon the story again this past week, the same week where I swung my fist angrily at many empty boats. Some situations, I believe, I actually made worse because of my reactions. In fact, they weren't even actual situations *until* I reacted! As a comedian once said, I could kick my own ass.

Before beating myself up too much about it, though, I paused and realized that this is all part of our process. We are always surrounded by empty boats careening at reckless speeds into our emotional, mental, and professional lives, and, frankly, for many of us, those three lives are all the same. It becomes about reacting to things that are real, not to things that make us feel a certain way. It is separating our facts from our fears. It is about accepting our anxiousness for the future and understanding that it has absolutely nothing to do with what will happen in next minute. Because we don't know that.

Be thankful for your empty boats, as they carry one of the most valuable insights: your personal fear. My boat is different than your boat. The boat represents your issues, your scars, your past. It is entirely possible to live your life swinging at shadows, taking actions based on some vague anxiety about the future. Many people spend years fighting for security – no matter what the price. When you step into entrepreneurship, though, you have to understand why you are driven and what motivates you. It is the key to success, as someone who doesn't know why they are getting up in the morning, sacrificing their time, and risking their livelihood for something will not be an entrepreneur for very long. Others may have the luxury of clinging to routine, repetition, and stability to keep their fears at bay. We do not have that option. As a result, the moments where we can see, feel, and identify our fears are truly gifts to our future selves.

"Fear is often an indicator that you're going in the right direction," *Unmistakable* author Srinivas Rao puts it. "It repeatedly indicates your next new level."

Do you know what you are afraid of now? Congratulations. Now you know your pain point, the area where you need to grow, and that knowledge will get you a step closer to mastering yourself. It is an insight people who never take the entrepreneurial journey will rarely understand.

YOUR NEXT STEP

Come enjoy my free videos,
insightful articles, and more at
www.bitesized.biz.

And if you're ready to join the *BITE-SIZED ENTREPRENEUR* conversation, our
budding online community is where
bite-sized entrepreneurs like yourself
can connect with each other, get
exclusive content and even get an
opportunity to talk one-on-one with me
to help steer you closer to your goals.

It is the Ultimate Bite-Sized
Entrepreneur Community at
www.paylancing.com.

Choose the GOOD subscription, type in
GETSTARTEDTODAY, and you'll get
half off community access and an
opportunity to consult with me.

I look forward to connecting with you!

SIGNIFICANT QUOTES & REFERENCES

- Table of Contents
  - Opening quote: Mihaly Csikszentmihalyi, "The Roots of Discontent", from *Flow* (Harper & Row, 1990)
- Chapter 1: Create Limitations
  - Opening quote: Peter Sims, "Failing Quickly to Learn Fast", from *Little Bets* (Simon & Schuster, 2011)
  - Sleeping quote: *Slumberwise*, "Your Ancestors Didn't Sleep Like You". Originally published May 16, 2013
  - Maria Popova reference: *Brain Pickings*, "Why Time Slows Down When We're Afraid, Speeds Up as We Age, and Gets Warped on Vacation". Originally published May 16, 2013

- Adapted from the *Inc.* columns "Waking Up at 3 Every Morning Made Me Super Productive – Until It Didn't" and "What Having No Time At All Taught Me About Productivity". Originally published July 2, 2015 & July 30, 2015, respectively
- Chapter 2: Know Your Core
  - Martha Stewart quote: "Ask Yourself, What's the Big Idea?", from *The Martha Rules*. (Rodale, 2005)
- Chapter 3: Death By Networking
  - Adapted from the *Inc.* column "Why Too Much Networking Will Make You Less Productive". Originally published August 9, 2016
- Chapter 4: Write It Down
  - Adapted from the *Inc.* columns "The Power of

Writing, Not Typing, Your Ideas" and "The Scientific Reason Why You Are Smarter When You Write". Originally published August 7, 2015 & April 28, 2016, respectively

- Chapter 5: Empty Your Schedule
  - o Adapted from the *Inc.* column "Why You Need to Add a 'Blank Day' to Your Calendar". Originally published December 18, 2015
- Chapter 7: Walk It Out
  - o Adapted from the *Inc.* column "How Walking Can Make You a Better Entrepreneur". Originally published August 31, 2015
- Chapter 8: Stop Measuring Time
  - o Pema Chodron quote: "Commitment", *from Comfortable With Uncertainty* (Shambhula, 2003)

- Chapter 9: Do Less With More Impact
    - Opening quote: Steven Pressfield, "The Professional Does Not Wait for Inspiration", from *Turning Pro* (Black Irish Entertainment, 2012)
    - Adapted from the *Inc.* column "Why Being Productive All the Time is a Fool's Errand". Originally published June 16, 2016
- Chapter 11: Alternate Tasks
    - Adapted from the *Inc.* column "How to Boost Your Productivity by Adding 'Palate Cleansers' to Your Day". Originally published November 18, 2015
- Chapter 12: Overextending Yourself
    - Adapted from the *Inc.* column "4 Surefire Ways

to Avoid Overextending Yourself". Originally published June 2, 2016

- Chapter 13: Mastering Time
  - Adapted from the *Inc.* column "3 Ultimate Insider Tips from a Time Management Master". Originally published May 31, 2016
- Chapter 14: Put the Coffee Down
  - Adapted from the *Inc.* column "Why 11 am Coffee Makes You More Productive". Originally published September 23, 2015
- Chapter 15: Know Your Prime Time
  - Adapted from the *Inc.* column "Not Productive Enough? Here's a Smart Way to Fix the Problem". Originally published March 14, 2016

- Chapter 17: Opting Out
  - Opening quote: Mihaly Csikszentmihalyi, "Overview", from *Flow* (Harper & Row, 1990)
  - Rembert Brown quote: *Vulture*, "What Andre 3000 Taught Frank Ocean". Originally published August 25, 2016.
- Chapter 18: Looking for a Crisis
  - Steven Pressfield quotes: "Resistance and self-dramatization" and "Resistance and trouble", both from *The War of Art* (Black Irish Entertainment 2012)
  - Mark Suster quote: *Both Sides of the Table*, "Do You Suffer from the Urgency Addiction? It's More Common Than You Think". Originally published August 18, 2010.
  - Adapted from the *Inc.*

column "An Addiction
Most Entrepreneurs Have
– and How to Manage It".
Originally published June
16, 2016
- Chapter 19: Less, Better Email
  - Adapted from the *Inc.*
    column "The 1 Powerful
    Rule That Will
    Revolutionize Your
    Email". Originally
    published May 10, 2016
- Chapter 20: Creating "Me" Time
  - Adapted from the *Inc.*
    column "3 Powerful Ways
    You Can Make 'Me'
    Time". Originally
    published January 12, 2016
- Chapter 22: Silence Is Golden
  - Duke University quote:
    Nautilus, Daniel A. Gross,
    "This is Your Brain on
    Silence". Originally
    published August 21, 2014.
  - Adapted from the *Inc.*
    column "Want to Boost

135

Your Brain Power? Get Silent". Originally published March 29, 2016

- Chapter 23: Bulletproof
  - o Seth Godin quote: *The Tim Ferriss Show*, "Seth Godin on How to Think Small to Go Big",.Originally aired August 3, 2016
- Chapter 24: Shadowboxing
  - o Pema Chodron quote: "The Empty Boat", *from Comfortable With Uncertainty* (Shambhula, 2003)
  - o Srinivas Rao quote: *Creative Warriors Podcast*, "Srini Rao – Be Unmistakable". Originally aired August 30, 2016

ACKNOWLEDGMENTS

Thanks to the continued feedback and support from Randy Dotinga, Evelyn Kane, Chia Hwu, E. B. Boyd, Atul Techchandani, Mihad Ali, and Andrea King Collier, as well as my editor/goal-buddy/friend Jeanette Hurt and cover artist Bec Loss.

A big hat-tip to Peter Sims, Steven Pressfield, and Mihaly Csikszentmihalyi for heavily influencing this volume, as well as to Liz Funk and Laura Vanderkam for being both amazingly quotable and awesome supporters.

The Bite-Sized Entrepreneur series was inspired by my Inc. column Sane Success, so lots of gratitude to *Inc. Magazine*'s Laura Lorber, Douglas Cantor, and Kevin Ryan for supporting the growth of our column.

Most importantly, a big thanks to my entrepreneurial parents Bernadette

Johnson and David Brown, and my wife, Dr. Parul Patel, as well as our precocious boys Alec and Abhi. I love you.

About the Author

Damon Brown is a long-time journalist and author of several books, most notably *Our Virtual Shadow: Why We Are Obsessed with Documenting Our Lives Online* (TED Books 2013) and *Porn & Pong: How Grand Theft Auto, Tomb Raider and Other Sexy Games Changed Our Culture* (Feral House 2008), as well as the coffeetable book *Playboy's Greatest Covers* (Sterling Publishing 2012). THE PRODUCTIVE BITE-SIZED ENTREPRENEUR is his 19th book and the follow-up to the best-selling THE BITE-SIZED ENTREPRENEUR.

Damon co-founded the social meetup app Cuddlr while being the primary caretaker to his infant. It went number one on the Apple App store twice, changing the cultural conversation around platonic intimacy. The app was acquired less than a year after it launched, and the whirlwind experience inspired Damon's popular *Inc.com* column Sane Success as well as *THE BITE-SIZED ENTREPRENEUR*.

You can catch Damon in *Playboy*, *Fast Company*, and *Entrepreneur*, as well as at any locale that serves really spicy food. He lives in Southern California with his wife, two young sons, and bottles of hot sauce.

Connect with him at www.damonbrown.net or on Twitter at @browndamon.

Made in the USA
Charleston, SC
07 December 2016